VISITORS FROM THE RED PLANET

OTHER BOOKS BY DR. CRYPTON

Dr. Crypton and His Problems

Timid Virgins Make Dull Company and Other Puzzles, Pitfalls, and Paradoxes

VISITORS FROM THE RED PLANET

AND 76 OTHER SOLVE–THEM–YOURSELF MYSTERIES

Dr. Crypton

ILLUSTRATED BY
Gary Baseman

W·W· NORTON & COMPANY

New York · London

© 1990, 1987, Dr. Crypton
© 1988, 1989 United Feature Syndicate

Printed in the United States of America.

The text of this book is composed in Bodoni Book,
with display type set in Universe & Huxley Vertical.
Composition and manufacturing by the Maple-Vail Book
Manufacturing Group. Book design by Guenet Abraham.

First Edition

Library of Congress Cataloging-in-Publication Data

Dr. Crypton, 1956–
Visitors from the red planet and 76 other solve-them-
yourself mysteries / by Dr. Crypton.
    p.   cm.
1. Literary recreations.   2. Puzzles.   I. Title.
GV1493.D67   1990
793.73—dc20   89–26476

ISBN 0-393-30690-9

W. W. Norton & Company, Inc.
500 Fifth Avenue, New York, N.Y. 10110
W. W. Norton & Company Ltd.
37 Great Russell Street, London WC1B 3NU

1 2 3 4 5 6 7 8 9 0

TO ISAAC FOREBRAIN

Contents

Shades of Plutarch   **1**

Light of My Life   **3**

The Unbearable Truth   **5**

The General Who Bombed Out   **7**

The Sad Case of Ziegfried Hofstader   **9**

New Beesness   **11**

A Hair-Raising Call   **13**

The Strange Case of Maxie Gulp   **15**

Shades of Galileo   **17**

Signs of Genius   **19**

Bringing Home the Bacon   **21**

Time for Royalty   **23**

Truth Is the Strangest Lie   **25**

The Case of the Goo-Gooing Gourmet   **27**

Direct Hit   **29**

What's in a Name?   **31**

Hungry for Love   **33**

Weighty Decisions   **35**

Boxed into a Corner   **37**

Talking Back   **39**

Blind Date   **41**

Smoking Gun   **43**

The Case of the Computer Virus   **45**

Altered States   **47**

The Recondite Epistle   **49**

The Case of the Touching Balls   **51**

Rock and Roll Alibi   **53**

Bright Lights, Big Slip   **55**

Unearthing a Kingsize Error   **57**

Life and Death in the Jungle   **59**

First Impressions   **61**

Overtures in the Park   **63**

Why the Lobster Blushed   **65**

Questioned to Death   **67**

Prestidigitation   **69**

Out to Launch   **71**

The Hot Goods of Einstein Ferraro   **73**

Stupid Pet Tricks   **75**

Dreaming Is for the Birds   **77**

Darkness at Noon   **79**

Venngeance   **81**

The Case of the Three Witches   **83**

What a Woman Wants   **85**

Behind the Eight Ball   **87**

Throwing in the Towel   **89**

Secrets of the Orient   **91**

A Scrambled Affair   **93**

Coming of Age   **95**

Booked any Good Reds Lately?   **97**

Utter Nonsense   **99**

A Weighty Problem   **101**

I Am Curious Yellow   **103**

The Case of the Balanced Meal   **105**

Sailor's Delight   **107**

A Bad Case of Tunnel Vision   **109**

The River's Rude Surprise   **111**

Moonlighting   **113**

When Rain Comes between Mother and Child   **115**

The Case of the Slimy Stranger   **117**

Spaced Out   **119**

Fishy Nightmare   **121**

The Case of the Runaway Microwave   **123**

Visitors from the Red Planet   **125**

The Case of the Enigmatic Inscription   **127**

Just Dessert   **129**

An Olympic Lie   **131**

Picking Up the Pieces   **133**

Games People Play   **135**

Six-Legged Folks   **137**

Is There Room for Cuteness in This World?   **139**

The Twisted Tale of Mort Gore   **141**

The Case of the Roasted Rodent   **143**

The Dream That Boomeranged   **145**

Damn Lies   **147**

Eastern Wisdom   **149**

Big Apple Census   **151**

Gore Shows His Hand   **153**

VISITORS FROM THE RED PLANET

Shades of plutarch

I'm Dr. Crypton, master of the truth and destroyer of lies. I've spent the past two days in the tree house I call my branch office tackling the central question in the mathematics of mortality. If two wrongs don't make a right, is there a number N such that N wrongs do? I had almost proved that seven wrongs make a right when my train of thought was derailed by a loud knock on the tree house door. There radiating beauty as well as a high three-digit I.Q. was my old flame Josephine Forebrain and her brilliant toddler, Isaac.

"Crypy," she cooed. "It is clear that young Isaac will soon be the smartest man in the world. You'll have to settle for second place."

"Nonsense, my dear." I leaned closer to study the child. His nose was running, and he smiled broadly as he scratched his behind. "He does not look like a young Einstein," I said.

"Not a young Einstein," she replied. "But a young Plutarch!"

"A historian? How can that be?"

"Try him," she challenged.

I reached in my desk and extracted a list of the presidents in order, just their names, no other details. I gave the list to Isaac. "Josephine," I said, "I trust you to think up a question about the presidents."

"Isaac," she said, "by some cosmic coincidence, three of the first five presidents died on the Fourth of July. Can you name one?"

"James Monroe," replied the child. "I know for sure."

"You're right," Josephine said. "See, a historical genius." She beamed and, to my jealous dismay, planted a big soggy kiss on his cheek.

"Josephine," I said, "there's another explanation." What is it?

Light of my life

Poor Josephine. She's been down in the dumps ever since I exposed Isaac's knowledge of James Monroe. "He's not a young Plutarch," she wept.

Isaac's ribbing didn't help matters. "Mommy, I know history," he'd say, "I'll impress Crypton. Ask me when the Fourth of July is."

And yet, although I'd never admit it to her, something about the three-year-old's precocious humor signaled an awesome intelligence not unlike my own. Why, I wondered, wouldn't she tell me the identity of his father?

The three of us were in my tree house. Isaac was crouched over, watching a large ant haul a struggling beetle. Suddenly, the wind whistled and the tree house began to rock, first a little but gradually more and more.

Isaac beamed. "Simple harmonic motion?" he said.

"Yes, that's right," I said. I thought of the days long past when his mother and I engaged in a little s.h.m. of our own.

As the wind gusted, the bulb in the ceiling fixture flickered and then went out, plunging us into nearly total darkness. Isaac clutched his mother's legs. "It's a power failure," said Josephine. "What are we going to do?"

"Stay calm," I said. In the darkness, I watched Isaac reach into his mother's handbag and extract a pack of Life Savers. She spun around and slapped him.

"You kleptomaniac!" she shouted.

"Wintergreen!" he said, chewing one of them loudly. I had to restrain her from slapping him again.

"No, no," I said. "He's only trying to help." How?

The unbearable truth

When the power came back on, I looked at the mail. The first letter was from a distant correspondent.

"Dear Dr. Crypton, I'm writing from Antarctica. It's November, when the sun shines 24 hours a day and the wind gusts to 100 miles an hour. What is life like on the fifth largest continent? Well, we amuse ourselves by looking for identical snowflakes. And we eat a lot of frozen food. Good humor is what keeps us going.

"Antarctica, however, is not a backward place. The penguins lunched on sushi long before yuppies ever heard of the stuff. Sex here, however, is not for the birds. Emperor penguins mate only once a year. Imagine if one of them has a headache!

"This place is rough, though. Bears blend right into the landscape. Once, while fishing on an ice-free lake, I was caught in a blizzard. Half a ton of bear, with paws a foot wide, charged out of the blinding snow. I had a tranquilizer gun, but wasn't sure if it was strong enough. I blasted the bear full of drugs. The beast wailed and lumbered to a stop. That's all. Sincerely, Miles Remington."

Well, folks, Miles may have learned that safety comes in numb bears. His letter, however, contains a lie—which you must expose. What?

The general who bombed out

The second letter I read was from a war hero.

"Dear Dr. Crypton, I want to speak my mind before there are none of us World War I veterans left. You youngsters may laugh, but there was a time when men were proud to be soldiers. In 1925 I received a medal. The inscription said, 'for distinguished service in World War I.'

"Today, no one gives a hoot about war medals. War is too mechanized, with MAD and SMART and MIRV and SAM. It's machine against machine.

"When we fought, it was man against man. In World War I, bombs were even thrown by hand out of aircraft. We had to rely on ourselves. Going into the war, we had fewer than 60 planes. And we never had a tank. Old-fashioned combat made men of us all. Sincerely yours, General Malcolm Dewey."

Well, folks, I'd be more inclined to hear the general out if he were shooting straight from the hip. But he slipped up. How?

The sad case of ziegfried hofstader

I was so immersed in my mail that had a person of ordinary stature climbed into the tree house, I would not have noticed. But there's no escaping the arrival of the immense dog trainer Ziegfried Hofstader, who was breathing deeply and preparing to lower himself into my sturdiest easy chair. I like Zig. I admire true passion wherever it is manifested, and Zig has not one consuming passion but two: food and dogs. From his breast pocket he pulled out a glass vial of pea soup with mint cream and started to slurp it down. But his slurps were not as deafening as usual, so I knew something was wrong. Zig is painfully shy as well as proud—something the causal observer, watching him terrorize miniature schnauzers in the show ring, might not suspect.

"All is lost, Doctor!" he blubbered into his soup. "I've spent thousands on a championship purebred Chow Chow, but the animal's a loser. I've been laughed out of every show ring in the country. What can you do with an inferior show dog?"

"Eat it," I said, not totally in jest.

Zig brightened momentarily. "Yeah? I hear that woman who runs the Philippines likes to eat dog." Then he looked sad again. "Naw," he said, "I couldn't do that. Leo's too cute. He's always smiling at me with his cute dark eyes and his little pink tongue hanging out."

"Why did you name him Leo?" I asked.

"'Cause he looks like a lion."

"What's his disposition like?"

"He's aloof with everyone except me."

"Where did the breed originate?"

"In China, at least 2,000 years ago."

I smiled. "Zig, you've been taken for a ride." How?

New beesness

While Ziegfried stalked off to pout, I read another letter. It was from a woman driver.

"Dear Dr. Crypton, May this story serve as a warning to other nature lovers. I was driving along a parkway in New England when I spied a lush meadow. I pulled over to the side and got out. I ran through fields of blooming thistle, goldenrod, and black-eyed Susan.

"When I dropped to my knees and pressed my nostrils to the summer flowers, I felt a sharp prick in the lobe of my right ear. It was the sting not of Cupid's arrow but of a yellow jacket. You know, the pesky yellow-and-black wasp that nests in the ground. Using the mirror in my make-up kit, I resourcefully extracted the stinger with a pair of tweezers from my Swiss Army knife.

"I'm allergic to wasps but my epinephrine pills were back in the car. I coughed and wheezed as I ran back—just in the nick of time. Even in this country people die each year from insect stings. I narrowly avoided becoming another statistic. Best wishes, Amanda Bloom."

Well, folks, there's something that takes the sting out of Ms. Bloom's story. What is it?

A hair—raising call

While I was penning a stinging rebuke to Amanda Bloom, the phone rang. It was Harrison Tweed, Capitol Hill lobbyist for the South Korean toupee industry. He is not one of my favorite people. Indeed, he is downright fawning and garrulous. And he's pitifully bad at snooker. Still, I accepted his collect call.

"Doctor!" he exclaimed. "That article on how psychosis did in the dinosaurs was nothing short of brilliant! A Nobel is surely around the corner! In fact, I shall nominate you myself!"

"Thank you Tweed," I replied, "but get to the point." I am a busy man.

"I'm in San Francisco. At a huge gathering of scientists, and I've sat in on the lectures."

"Science," I said. "What do you know about science?"

"It's not the science I've come for but the hairstyles of the scientists. People loved Einstein's hair. I'm looking for the new Einstein, someone brainy whose hair I can turn into a toupee for the smart set. But listen Crypton, that's not why I'm calling. I've learned a lot of science while I'm here. Quite frankly, I'm worried about you."

"Why?" I asked.

"You've heard of chaos? The new nonlinear mathematics that rules the universe?"

"Of course I've heard of it. I helped pioneer it, with my work on Jupiter's Great Red Spot."

"Right. How could I forget? Surely, the folks in Stockholm will recognize that work."

"Stop fawning, Tweed," I said, "and tell me what's wrong with my health."

"Well, remember those EKG's and EEG's of yours that you showed me? The beats weren't exactly regular. You were even proud that they showed chaotic behavior. Well, I hate to tell you, but chaotic heartbeats and brain waves are a sign of pathology. The world is going to hell in a hand basket, and so are you."

"Tweed," I said, "I've heard enough. You're as misinformed as ever." Why?

The strange case of maxie gulp

Phone calls from Tweed always put me in a foul mood. To recover, I climbed down from the tree house and went off to Bozman's for a drink. There I was leaning against the long bar nursing a friendly glass of aging grape juice, dreaming of a time long ago. . . . The swollen purple nose of Maxie Gulp bore no resemblance to my vision, but at least he talked. Memories don't talk. Or at least if they talk, I ain't listening.

"Doc," said Gulp, "let me be frank. I need a drink and I'm broke. Advance me some cash and win a friend for life."

"Maxie," I said, "I consider you my friend already. There is no need for you to test that friendship. You earned it long ago."

"Doc," he said, "you are a hard man. There is nothing of the soft touch in you. I respect that. I am like you. I don't want nothing for nothing. I shall earn my sustenance. I'll make you a friendly wager. Answer me this simple question. Why do firemen wear red suspenders?"

"To hold their pants up," I said. "No drink."

Maxie's face fell. Clearly he had not anticipated my clever retort. Then his face brightened. In fact, his nose actually glowed. "Best two out of three?" he asked.

"Fine," I said. "Only this time, I do the asking. Go stand with your left side against the wall. Keep your left foot, left knee, left hip, left shoulder, and left cheek firmly against the wall. Then lift your right leg off the floor."

Maxie happily hurried off to comply with my simple request, and I finished the rest of my drink in peace. I left soon afterwards without seeing any more of my friend.

Why did Maxie leave me in peace?

Shades of galileo

I staggered home from Bozman's. In my partially inebriated condition, I could not make it up to my treetop office, so I went inside the house and fell asleep. When I woke, it was daylight. After a pot of Jamaican Blue Mountain coffee, I decided to work on my project of translating English limericks into Kurdish. I was in the middle of a particularly profound limerick when I heard tiny footsteps on the roof. Squirrels, I thought, and I returned to the line: "An amoeba name Sam and his brother." I gazed out the window as I pondered how I was going to translate amoeba. But my concentration was suddenly disturbed by a cannonball and musket ball whizzing past the windowpane and landing, with a loud thud, on my prize geraniums. Fuming, I raced outside. There, teetering on the edge of the roof, was little Isaac.

"Isn't *he* the young Galileo," said a melodious voice on the ground, the unmistakable voice of the boy's mother, Josephine Forebrain.

"I suppose," I said.

"He knows everything about physics," she said.

"Everything?" I said.

"Yes, Uncle Crypton," the boy said. "Mommy thinks a heavy ball falls faster than a light one. She's dumb. In a vacuum they fall at the same rate."

"Tell me, Isaac, if you rolled two balls down a sloped board, would they also reach the end at the same time?"

"No, not necessarily."

"One last question: Who invented wax paper?"

"Thomas Edison, of course."

I started to smile, "Josephine, I'm afraid your boy doesn't know everything about physics." What did I mean?

Signs of genius

Pity Josephine. She still hasn't recovered from my observing that her son Isaac knows as little about gravity as Galileo did. You think she'd be pleased to hear her son and the great Italian physicist mentioned in the very same sentence.

"So he's no Einstein," she said.

"Few of us are," I said.

"I do think he's a Sherlock Holmes."

"Holmes? Your little Isaac?" I stared incredulously at the boy as he crawled on all fours through my flower bed.

"Try him," she challenged.

"OK." I called to the child and he wheeled around, decapitating four geraniums. "Isaac, listen closely. I have a mystery for you. A farmer comes across a dead man in his corn field. The man is dead because his backpack contains something that should not be there. What does it contain?"

"That's easy," Isaac said. "A parachute."

"Very good. How about this one: A mother goes to a hardware store and selects some items from a bin labeled 50 cents. She gives her purchases to the cashier, who says, 'That will be one for 50 cents, twelve for a dollar, and one hundred for a dollar fifty. That comes to three dollars.' The woman was not taken aback. What did she buy?"

Isaac looked crushed. He obviously didn't know. Do you?

Bringing home the bacon

I do not particularly enjoy stumping small children. I enjoy stumping anyone. But it is tough being a paradoxologist; you open yourself up to people trying to stump you. Friends start being cryptic. Instead of sending Hallmark birthday greetings, they compose limericks about you, encrypt them, and then write them with smelly invisible ink. Sometimes a fellow just wants to hear a simple "Happy Birthday."

Last night I was a dinner guest at the home of Adrian Snork, curator of porcine fossils for the Idaho Pork Association. Snork knew that I was a master of the cryptic, and he lost no time making feeble stabs at being enigmatic.

"Ah," he said, waving a cocktail frank at a photo in his family album. "Brothers and sisters I have none. But this man's father is my father's son."

"It's your own son," I said reflexively, having heard the same puzzle when I was in diapers. I took a bite of pork chop smothered with bacon bits.

"Oh, a smart guy, eh?" said Snork, slurping up a mouthful of sausage soup. "Then how about the fellow in this picture? He's the only son of the only brother of the only aunt of my father's only niece."

"It must be you," I said. "Quite an old picture, I see."

Snork sucked in his huge gut and waved a sparerib at another photo. "Pretty, isn't she? She's the only niece of the father of the only cousin of the uncle of the only grandson of the brother of my cousin's mother."

I smiled because my computer-like brain immediately discerned who she was. Who?

Time for royalty

I really must hand it to Harrison Tweed. The man has no shame. Why only last week he nearly convinced the Louvre to fund a search for the Venus De Milo's missing arms. And the week before he was in New Delhi hawking sacred cows.

I accepted his collect call on my car phone as I sped across the Brooklyn Bridge to lunch at the River Cafe.

"Doctor!" he said. "I won't even try to sell you the bridge you're on."

"Tweed, get to the point." Life is too short for idle chitchat.

"I'm in London, Doctor, at Buckingham Palace. I snuck into the place, just like that intruder. The decor is quite nice, especially the dainty floral pattern on her majesty's sheets."

"You were in the queen's bedroom?"

"Not were, am. As we speak, I'm having breakfast by her bed. The queen's in the loo. She made me at home, Doctor, by telling me tidbits about our presidents. Why she said that George Washington had size 13 feet and was Robert E. Lee's third cousin twice removed. She also recalled how in 1940 the Division of Fine Arts at U.S.C. selected Ronald Reagan as the man with the most perfect figure. She even recited a limerick that Woodrow Wilson wrote: 'I sat next to the Duchess at tea. It was just as I feared it would be. Her rumblings abdominal. Were truly phenomenal. And everyone thought it was me!' "

I laughed appreciatively, even though I knew there was something bloody wrong with Tweed's story. What's the problem?

Truth is the strangest lie

Tweed's lying brought back memories of my exploits with other compulsive liars. You have undoubtedly heard of those mysterious islands where half the inhabitants always tell the truth and the other half always lie. Nobody seems to have actually visited one of these islands, but everyone knows of someone who has, someone who found himself at the fork in a road with a strange islander (who could be either a truth teller or a liar) and who was able to ask only one question to find the right path.

That's simple. So is the case where the islanders don't speak English and you have to interpret their response. It's even possible to find the right road if half of them are zombies or psycho killers and you are armed with one silly question.

I once found myself on an island that made those places look like Romper Room. Picture, if you will, the Isle of Row, a one-acre forsaken swatch of desert in the middle of the Sea of Troubles. Despite its diminutive size, Row has no less than four kinds of people, all outwardly indistinguishable from one another. There are the members of the First Family, who always tell the truth, and the Pretenders, who never do. There are the Eccentrics, who may or may not tell the truth, depending on whim. Finally there are the Wimps, who are incapable of speaking unless they have heard one of the other kinds of people speak, and then they obsequiously chime in.

One day, as luck would have it, I found myself at the only crossroads on the island, facing four possible routes. Three Rowians stood by, milling about, and I had only two damn questions to ask in order to reach, as directly as possible, the fabled hundred-foot Tower of Schmooze, the island's premier, albeit only, tourist attraction. What did I do?

The case of the goo-gooing gourmet

The view from atop the Tower of Schmooze was so spectacular I could do nothing but wax poetic. I pulled out a pad and finished the lyrics of my latest musical, "Archimedes on the Beach." But even there, in the middle of nowhere, my portable cellular phone let out a loud noise. Compulsive as I am, I answered on the first ring.

It was, courtesy of fiber optics, the soft, melodious voice of Josephine Forebrain. "Crypy," she cooed, "Isaac has surprised me again. You were right; my three-year-old is not a young Einstein, a young Holmes, or a young Plutarch. But you misjudged him. He does have precocious talent. He's a young Julia Child!"

"A young Child? How can that be? Cooking requires extraordinary aesthetic sophistication that a tyke, even yours, couldn't possibly possess."

"No, Crypton. You're mistaken. He's a veritable songbird in the kitchen, although he needs to stand on four phone books to reach the burners. He can turn the simplest ingredients into Epicurean delights. His forte is desserts. Why just last night he made a flaky pie crust from 6 tablespoons of chilled butter, 2 cups of flour, a teaspoon of salt, 4 tablespoons of vegetable shortening, and a third of a cup of cold water. The day before he added fresh kiwifruit to Jell-O. The result was divine. You'd bite into the soft Jell-O only to be surprised by the kiwi treat hiding inside."

I shook my head sadly. Why?

Direct hit

Upon returning to the States from the Isle of Row, I survived a most harrowing experience. I am a better man for it, however, and I hope that by sharing the experience you too will benefit.

I was playing cards on an old-time riverboat, the kind that used to ply the great trade routes up and down the Mississippi. Seated across the green felt table from me was the notorious gambler and hooligan Montague Sidewinder. I had just drawn to my second inside straight, thoroughly cleaning out the Sidewinder fortune. He pretended not to care, but I knew that inside he was seething.

"Nice, doc," he said, "very nice. How about you cut the cards for double or nothing?"

"Sure," I said. "What's the game?"

"Not cards, exactly," he said with a dreadful sneer, "I propose a little mind game. You're famous for your mind games, are you not?"

"Indeed, I am."

"Tear a card in half," he said. "Then rip the resulting pieces in half again. Do this fifty times. Then stack all the scraps in a column."

"Gladly," I said, and I did so. It took me quite some time, and the resulting stack was a bit higher than even I was expecting, but so help me, I did it. Montague was outraged. He leapt to his feet, murder flashing in his evil yellow eyes.

"Why you mountebank, you wizard, you sorcerer!" he shouted. He pulled out his infamous pearl-handled revolver and fired point-blank at my chest. Naturally, I survived without a scratch.

How?

What's in a name?

The place I woke up in was Josephine's kitchen. She was reading a cookbook and Isaac was standing on a stool so that he could reach the counter. He had just finished melting baker's chocolate and was scooping it, with his dirty fingers, into a mixing bowl.

"What are you making?" Josephine inquired, as she pinched the boy's chocolate-smudged cheek.

"I'm going to make a chocolate berry tart," Isaac said. For a three-year-old, Isaac makes wicked deserts.

"Yum!" Josephine exclaimed. "What kind of berries are you going to use?"

"Loganberries. I picked them up at the gourmet market down the street." The tot is a mother's dream. Not only does he cook, he shops too.

"Ah, the loganberry," I said, making a feeble effort to join the conversation. "The loganberry is my favorite fruit because it's an eponym."

"Huh? An epo what?" Josephine said.

"An eponym—*nym* as in *nym*phomaniac," I said.

"What's an eponym?" she said.

"An eponym is a word based on a person's name. The word loganberry comes from James Harvey Logan, a California Superior Judge, who grew the first such berries in the 1880s in Santa Cruz."

"Neat! Is that an eponym?" said Isaac, pointing to some Bibb lettuce on his mother's plate.

"How did you know?" I said. "During the decade before the Civil War, Major John B. Bibb developed the small, delicate Bibb lettuce in his backyard in Frankfort, Kentucky."

"Crypton!" said Josephine. "You're too much."

"And there's even an eponym in there," I said, peering into the gooey chocolate mixture that Isaac was stirring. "And it's not pasteurized milk I'm thinking of." What *was* I thinking of?

Hungry for love

It was chocolate city at the Forebrain's house. Josephine was sipping a cup of hot chocolate and Isaac was completing his chocolate berry tart.

"Ah, chocolate," Josephine said. "It's amazingly addictive."

"It is good," I said, "but there's no pharmacological evidence that it's addictive."

"Oh, fudge, you're always shooting things down."

"I am a man of science, Josephine, and I can't help correcting misinformation. You'll be happy to know, though, that there is some chemical evidence that chocolate is good for you. The sweet contains stearic acid, which seems to lower cholesterol."

"That's neat. But I must confess, Crypy, that I eat chocolate because I'm love-starved."

"You're what?"

"Love-starved. I eat chocolate because I read in some women's magazine that it contains a brain chemical that gives you the same high as being in love."

"Oh, you mean monoamine oxidase inhibitor. It does give you a high, but there's not enough of it in chocolate to do the trick."

"There you go again—shooting things down."

Isaac was tugging at her hemline. "Mommy, did I hear you say that you're love-starved? I have just the answer." Isaac presented her with a tart, but first he made a big show of crumbling graham crackers on it.

What was the tyke up to?

Weighty decisions

Having consumed the graham crackers, Josephine Forebrain was positively radiant. She was dancing about the kitchen, humming softly. "I haven't felt so good in years," she said, planting a juicy kiss on Isaac's ruddy cheeks.

I know I should hardly be jealous of a mother fondly kissing her three-year-old child, but I couldn't help it. I thought back to the days when Josephine and I were a hot item.

"Crypy," she cooed. "I'm going to make you two of your favorite treats, pasta with a creamy arugula sauce and blueberries with whipped cream." She had already prepared the ingredients. The bitter arugula greens were finely chopped on a cutting board. Next to the board were two measuring cups that looked identical, each half filled with cream.

Josephine put some salt and a dab of olive oil in a pot of water and set it on the stove to boil. She turned to the two measuring cups. "Drat!" she said. "I forgot which one's the heavy cream and which one's the light cream."

"Does it really matter?" the tyke inquired.

"It's not so important which cream I put on the pasta. But it is for the blueberries. Only the heavy cream will whip."

"Well, then," said Isaac, "let's see which is heavier." The child climbed on a stool so that he could reach the counter. He picked up a cup in each hand. "This one's heavier."

"You brainy savior," Josephine said, giving him an even bigger kiss.

At that moment I butted in—it wasn't because I was jealous but because I needed to stop Josephine from ruining the meal.

Why exactly did I butt in?

Boxed into a corner

Josephine, Isaac, and I were savoring blueberries with whipped cream. The three-year-old made fun of his mother's blue tongue, and I went back for a third helping. Before I could dig in, the telephone rang. It was Harrison Tweed, calling from Texas.

"Doctor!" he said. "It's so good to hear your voice. I read your brilliant paper on the unification of the forces and wanted to offer my congratulations."

"Thank you," I said, somewhat cooly. I know from experience that whenever Tweed is handing out praise, he's about to ask for a big favor.

"I also wanted you to know that I was a hero today."

"You were?"

"A DC-10 crashed today near Houston. I happened to be at the scene. The investigators couldn't find the flight recorder among the wreckage. But, eagle eyes that I am, I found it. I spotted its dull blackness in some thick shrubbery. I retrieved it for them, and when they played back the tape of the cockpit conversation, they learned something disturbing: on a dare, the pilot had let the flight engineer—who wasn't certified to fly the plane—handle the takeoff. That decision turned out to be fatal."

I cut Tweed off before he could hit me up for a favor. "I don't believe a word you're saying. You were no hero today."

Why was I so sure?

Talking back

It felt good to show up Harrison Tweed. The nerve of him concocting a tall story about how he heroically recovered the black box from an airplane crash. I had hoped my exposing Tweed would win me brownie points with Josephine, but she and her little Forebrain had fallen asleep at the kitchen table.

I tiptoed by them for a fourth helping of blueberries with whipped cream. Klutz that I am, I knocked the bowl off the table, waking Josephine and Isaac.

The three-year-old rubbed his eyes and peered under the table. "Was it a rat I saw?" the boy asked.

Josephine looked under the table. "You're probably just dreaming. There's nothing there," she assured him. "Have some more berries." She refilled his bowl.

Isaac peered into the bowl. In the middle were two tiny bugs doing a kind of dance. "O gnats, tango!" he blurted out.

Josephine, too, looked into the bowl. "They do appear to be dancing but I wouldn't go so far as to call it a tango. More like a polka."

I chuckled to myself. How seriously she treated the child! If only she knew his special talent. What's the talent?

Blind date

Josephine and Isaac Forebrain had fallen back to sleep, so I decided it was a good time to catch up on my own mail. The first letter had no return address.

"Dear Dr. Crypton, I do not understand people who go abroad for vacations. America's balance of trade is so bad that I think we should be spending our money at home. And there are plenty of things to do here, too. I've never left the country, and I've had a blast.

"My favorite recreational activity is going to the local Playboy Club for dinner. The bunnies are just great in their electric blue or pink outfits with the cute fluffy tails. I particularly like the VIP room—VIP, by the way, stands for Very Important Playboy. The bunnies in the VIP room are foreign girls, and they serve a mean midnight supper. Tears come to my eyes when the piano bar plays the 'Playboy's Theme.' Some of the lyrics go, 'If your boy's a Playboy/Loosen your control./ If his eye meanders,/Sweet goose your ganders/Just one more ornery critter.'

"I know I'm old-fashioned. But even in this age of feminism, I can't help going to Playboy Clubs. In fact, I went just last night. Sincerely yours, Alf Burgess.'

Alf's seeming patriotism can't make up for the fact that he's a liar. How can I be so sure?

Smoking gun

The second letter I opened was from a distraught young woman.

"Dear Dr. Crypton, The oddest thing happened to me the other day. I was having dinner at my grandfather's in Kennesaw, Georgia, a town some 25 miles northwest of Atlanta. It was just he and grandma and me. Grandma served one of his favorite dishes: roast quail stuffed with crawfish corn bread dressing. She also served piping hot yam biscuits and braised okra. Grandpa was in heaven, and Grandma cranked the gramophone up and put on 'Tea for Two.' Although Grandpa is 95, he is as fit physically and mentally as a man half his age, and Grandma is pretty spry, too. The two of them danced around the room.

"When the record was over, they sat down, and somehow the conversation turned to guns. Grandpa explained that he had nothing against guns. Since I'm a liberal northerner, I was disturbed to hear that. I asked him whether he kept a gun in the house. He said no, and I was much relieved. But then Grandma's eyes filled with fire; she leapt from her rocker and told her husband that she was going to make a citizen's arrest of him! I need your help. I'm confused about what happened. Grandpa has never gotten so much as a parking ticket, let alone been arrested before. Is Grandma really off her rocker? Please help, Marie Winchester."

Well, Ms. Winchester, I'm afraid Grandma is entirely in her element. Why?

The case of the computer virus

Before I could finish the mail, my cellular phone rang. It was Tweed again.

"Fire away," I said.

"Our mainframe computer, which keeps track of our hairpiece orders, is infected by a deadly virus. So far the virus seems confined to three circuit boards. My plan is to have each of our three technicians—Alex, Bernie, and Clayton—remove one of the boards. The problem is that we are down to only two pairs of sterile gloves, and it takes two hands to remove a circuit board."

"Why is that a problem? They can simply share gloves."

"That would not be wise. This virus is so pernicious it can cross the man-machine barrier and infect a person. Indeed, it is possible one of the technicians is already infected. That is why they are avoiding touching each other or, for that matter, touching surfaces someone else has touched."

"So why involve all three technicians. Just have one or two of them remove all three circuit boards."

"That would be the easy way. But each technician is extremely insecure; each would be crushed if he couldn't remove a board. You've got to help me. I'm afraid that if the virus spreads to the computer's central processing unit, all our toupee orders will be scrambled. I don't want to end up sending a Mohawk hairpiece to a Wall Street banker."

Could I help Tweed out of his predicament?

Altered states

Having helped Tweed, I returned to the mail. The next letter was from those happy wanderers, Walt and Winny Bago, and their twins, Polly and Esther.

"Dear Dr. Crypton, We wanted a vacation spot that was not only hot but exciting. So we were rather disappointed when our travel agent sent us to Florida. How ordinary, we thought. What does the sunshine state offer besides beautiful beaches, fabulous fruit, and Disney World?

"Imagine how thrilled we were to find that the southernmost state in the union boasts the oldest national bird sanctuary, the world's first underwater park, and the second largest fresh-water lake in the U.S. We're also going to stop in St. Augustine, the oldest existing European settlement on the continent. But best of all, we're heading for the Tupperware Museum Gallery of Historical Food Containers, just south of Orlando. We can hardly contain ourselves.

"We think this trip will be the greatest thing since Ponce de Leon discovered Florida in 1513, while seeking the fountain of youth. Best wishes, the Bago family."

I'm afraid, folks, that Walt and Winny have been caught with their Ponce down. Not everything they've told me is the truth. What were they wrong about?

The recondite epistle

The last letter was from one of my most faithful correspondents, Ed Ho, an adventurous, sesquipedalian friend who freely uses seven-million-dollar words, compensating, I suppose, for his short name. His obscure vocabulary makes even William Buckley feel illiterate.

"Dear Dr. Crypton. I never thought I'd outdo my earlier untrowable culinary adventure in which we ate a mammock of defrosted mammoth. I must admit, it was rather manducable. It tasted surprisingly like chicken. In search of new taste sensations, I recently went on a fishing trip to Lake Chargoggagoggmanchaugagoggchaubunagungamaugg (an Indian name meaning "You fish on your side, I fish on my side; nobody shall fish in the middle'). The preantepenultimate fish I caught was a humuhumunukunukuapuaa, but showing encraty, I threw it back. For dinner I had moreta, which left me saprostomous. Still hungry, I settled for a toddick of lopadotemachoselachogaleokranioleipsanodrimhypotrimmatosilphioparaomelitokatekechymenokichlepikossyphophattoperisteralektryonoptekephalliokigklopeleiolagoiosiraiobaphetraganopterygon. What a meal it was! Sincerely, Ed Ho."

In the interest of hippopotomonstrosesquipedalian fun, Ho bent the truth. How?

The case of the touching balls

When I write to Ho, I make sure not to use any word that has more than three letters. But I was saved from composing a letter to him by the unexpected arrival of my athletic nephew Carl "Killer" Crypton.

I like to think that had I applied myself, I could have become a championship athlete, too. The evidence lies within Carl's huge, muscular body, which lets him be a pro linebacker by fall, a pro power forward by winter, and a designated hitter by summer. I share some of the killer's gene pool. His grandmother—my mother—was a defecting Bulgarian hammer throw champ.

It is always a treat to visit with the Killer, but today he seemed down.

When my talented nephew is depressed, everyone around him is affected, and not just because the professional football, basketball, and baseball player becomes 260 pounds of highly trained hostility. Carl is sensitive, and his hurt becomes your hurt.

Unfortunately, Carl is often hurt, owing to yet another of his many gifts; the man is an artist. He can draw and paint and decorate. His passion is design. Today, he had to design the cover of the press guide to his basketball team.

"Unk," he cried. "I have the job of a lifetime, but I can't pick up the ball and run with it. I want to put a basketball smack in the middle of the cover and surround it with as many basketballs as can possibly touch it."

"Six," I said helpfully. "The maximum number of same-size circles that can touch another circle is six."

"I know that," said the ungrateful relative. "Everyone knows that. I want something really special. I'm going to put a hologram on the cover. So I need to know *in three dimensions*, how many basketballs can come in contact with a given basketball."

That, too, was no sweat for me. I told Carl. His mind at ease, he went out and scored the first quintuple double in the history of the league.

How many balls did I tell Carl to use?

Rock and roll alibi

Carl "Killer" Crypton departed my place a happy man. I retired to the study in order to watch Vanna turn the letters on "Wheel of Fortune." Halfway through the first card a shrill high-tech beep punctuated the air. Was it the phone, the alarm clock, the oven timer, or a warning that the smoke-detector's batteries were low? The downside of the microelectronics revolution is that everything sounds the same. Another beep and I surmised it was the phone.

The oily voice on the other end was that of Harrison Tweed. He usually calls collect from some distant place; this time he was paying.

"Ah, doctor, good to reach you. It's a shame the Nobel committee passed you by. I think you deserve one, for predicting the new supernova long before anyone spotted it."

"Tweed," I said, "don't pander to me. I'm not some congressman you have to butter up."

"No, no. You have the wrong idea. It's just that I'm in Woodstock, New York, and last night the stars were so spectacular I was reminded of your astronomical observations."

"Woodstock? What are you doing there?"

"I'm at the site of that great festival of 1969, on the huge dairy farm. Remember Joplin, Hendrix, and Sebastian, all the greats who were there! 'The times they are a' changin'.'"

"Tweed, this is a pleasant surprise. What would your conservative employer think of your returning to the site of free love and free-flowing drugs?"

"South Korea knows I'm here. In fact, they sent me here. They want me to relive the time when hair was long. They plan to introduce bushy hairpieces."

"Tweed," I said. "I've had enough." I slammed down the phone in disgust. As always, he had told a lie. What?

Bright lights, big slip

Tweed may be a fraud, but I hardly expected Kepler Washington to be one too. The University of Toronto astronomer had written me:

"Dear Dr. Crypton, I was one of the first to see the now-famous supernova 1987A without a telescope. Without even binoculars. Just with my bare eyes. It was truly awesome. I think of 1987A as a grandparent since many chemical elements necessary for life on Earth, including human life, were forged in the blast furnaces of supernovas.

"The sight of 1987A brought me closer to our ancestors in another way. Imagine southern Africa some 170,000 years ago. Although it was cooler, familiar wildlife such as giraffes and baboons raced across the savanna. So did a menagerie of strange, extinct beasts like the giant buffalo whose horn span was longer than an entire buffalo is today. In this environment some of our stone-age ancestors may have stared at the cosmos and witnessed the cataclysmic death of the star whose light reached me, when I gazed up at the sky in February 1987.

"It's extraordinary to think that when we viewed supernova 1987A, we were seeing light that set out some 170,000 years ago. Sincerely yours, Kepler Washington."

Well folks, Washington shows admirable reverence for all of our ancestors, from mindless organic elements to stone-age troglodytes. But his science is less than stellar. Where did he slip up?

Unearthing a kingsize error

Harrison Tweed has no shame. You'd think the toupee industry lobbyist would crawl under a rock after I exposed his lack of knowledge of the Woodstock Festival. But no, Tweed is still up to his old, hair-brained tricks. Why just yesterday, while I was planting the last of my fall bulbs, I received a collect call from him on my cordless phone.

"Doctor!" the staticky voice boomed. "I'm in Egypt, in a small town near Giza where all those great pyramids are."

"Egypt? What are you doing there?" Surely the toupee business hasn't taken you there," I said as I gingerly sprinkled bone meal in the hole I was digging.

"No, not business. I'm here to pursue my avocation, archaeology."

"You, an archaeologist?" I could hardly disguise my contempt as I lowered a nascent tulip into the hole.

"I am a very good archaeologist. In fact, I've just made a monumental find. I've uncovered a new tomb, of a pharaoh who ruled from about 2662 to 2679 B.C. It's sure to upset the history books! And the riches I found in the sarcophagus make Imelda Marcos seem like a bag lady."

"Tweed," I said, "you are beneath contempt." As always, his ignorance had betrayed him. How?

Life and death in the jungle

Tweed's games were aggravating. I was so mad I decided to journey to a foreign land where no one could reach me. I headed to South America.

You could have knocked me over with a six-inch blowtorch when young Isaac Forebrain tugged on my coat and drooled on my shoe. Not that I was surprised he dribbled on my shoe; he was always drooling. I was surprised because I was on a tramp steamer navigating the mouth of the Amazon, and Isaac was presumably receiving private tutoring in Vienna from his mother, my erstwhile lover and intellectual rival, Josephine Forebrain.

"Hello, Isaac," I said, wiping my shoe on the back of his pants leg. "What in the world are you doing here?"

"Saving da world," said Isaac, who turned and went tearing off the deck. Our boat was docked at a tiny encampment in the heart of the jungle. I observed Isaac run down the gangplank and make for the dense underbrush. In close pursuit followed Josephine, shouting mild imprecations that he stop and think a little, for God's sake. Curious, I followed. When I caught up with them in a small clearing, Isaac was dancing madly about, stomping on a colony of small ants with his hiking boots. Josephine was trying vainly to restrain him.

"Honey dearest," she pleaded, "remember your oath to the World Naturalist League! On your sacred honor, you must harm no living thing that does not threaten you! What on earth do you have against these harmless little toilers?"

"Bad ants," screamed Isaac, who was becoming very hysterical. "Bad ants! Kill! Kill!"

"Josephine," I said gently, so as not to bruise her fragile ego, "while Isaac is exhibiting the excess enthusiasm of extreme youth, and while we may disapprove of his methods, there is method in his madness, which you would understand if you made even the slightest effort to keep up with the scientific press."

What did Isaac and I know that Josephine didn't?

First impressions

And it was not just Isaac and Josephine who caught up with me in the Amazon, but my mail too. A letter miraculously reached me from Ms. Taken, a young naturalist in East Africa.

"Dear Dr. Crypton, Even on this continent, news of the antics of your presidential candidates sometimes reaches us. Here, among Americans deep in the bush, Gary Hart is known as a womanizer, and no sage words about life-and-death issues could possibly salvage his tarnished image. When people label someone, however apt the label may be, it tends to obscure the rest of him.

"We treat animals the same way. Take the ostrich. They have gone down in history as creatures that ignore danger by burying their heads in the sand. That I have seen them do—and Gary Hart did date while separated from his wife—but that's not all they do. Why isn't the ostrich recognized instead as something singularly noble? It is, after all, the largest bird alive, standing more than 9 feet high and reaching 13 feet when running. Moreover, it's a marathoner; no other animal can match its 50-mile-per-hour speed for 30-minute stretches. Or why isn't the ostrich hailed for its sharp eyesight or its unique anatomical feature of having only two toes on each foot? Or, like Hart, why aren't male ostrichs branded as womanizers, because they truly are polygamous? Sincerely yours, Iva B. Taken."

Well, Ms. Taken has embellished her story. How?

Overtures in the park

A second letter managed to get through to me in the wilds of South America. It was from Clara Nett of Pie Town, Nevada.

"Dear Dr. Crypton, A few years ago my family shared a very special moment on Boston Common. The occasion was an outdoor concert of Peter Ilyich Tchaikovsky's *1812 Overture*. We brought with us a picnic lunch of cold chicken and a bottle of Johnnie Walker Red Label.

"Since the Common is the nation's oldest public park, it was the perfect place to hear a historic piece of music. Even the kids liked the concert, particularly when the cannons were fired, as Tchaikovsky had called for. I'm a Tchaikovsky fan, and I enjoyed it even more than his other classics, *Swan Lake* and *Nutcracker Suite*. The climax took my breath away. How wonderful, I thought, that a Russian had composed such a splendid tribute to an American military victory. If only Gorbachev was that magnanimous!

"Later I learned that Tchaikovsky was not always that receptive to foreigners. As a child, Tchaikovsky is said to have kissed a map of Russia and then spat on the other countries. His nurse, who witnessed this rude behavior, pointed out that she herself was French. 'I know,' he said, 'That's why I covered France with my hand.' Yours, Clara Nett."

I'm afraid that Ms. Nett is not as knowledgeable as she thinks. What is her mistake?

Why the lobster blushed

Since the Amazon hardly proved to be a retreat from civilization, I returned home to the full amenities of flush toilets and Häagen Dazs ice cream. My first morning back was gloriously sunny, and I intended to spend it reading in the basement, safe from the sun's cancerous rays. But my intentions were foiled by the unexpected arrival of Josephine and her toddler Isaac.

"Josephine," I said, "you know I don't like surprises."

"I know. But it couldn't be helped. We have something to discuss. It's about Isaac." She smiled sweetly, and my skin tingled; at last, I thought, she'd reveal the identity of the boy's father. Josephine guided young Isaac into my study, where he quickly became absorbed with programming my Macintosh® to display fractal patterns. We left him there and returned to the foyer.

"Crypton," she said, "you are giving him a complex."

"What?"

"Yes, every time we're here, you have to upstage him. You've shot down his knowledge of history, his understanding of physics, his mimicking of Holmes. Remember, Isaac is only a three-year-old. I know he'll grow up to be the smartest of Earth's creatures, including dolphins and talking chimps. But for now, treat him like a child."

"Goo, goo, goo, goo, goo," I practiced.

"Crypton, knock it off. You can still talk to him. Just don't ask him a question you wouldn't even ask of a post-doc."

"OK, I'll ask him kids' stuff." I called to the next room: "Isaac, why is the Prince of Wales like a gorilla but not like a bald man and an orphan?"

"Crypton," Josephine said. "You're being stupid." But her protests were drowned out by Isaac's giggling. He knew the answer to the riddle even if she didn't. Do you?

Questioned to death

"hy is a wife like a newspaper?" three-year-old Isaac asked.

"Well," I paused, pretending to think, not wanting Isaac to feel that I knew the answer to every riddle, even though I did. "I suppose a wife is like a newspaper because a man shouldn't take his neighbor's."

Isaac frowned. He was eager to stump me. "What's the difference," he squealed, "between a cat and a comma?"

"Oh, I don't know," I said.

"I don't believe you."

"OK, I know." I'm not very good at lying. "A cat has its claws at the end of its paws and a comma has its pause at the end of its clause."

"Enough!" shouted Josephine. "When I told you to treat Isaac like a child, I never expected you to descend to this."

"Descend? Riddles are hardly descending. You should know that riddles have altered the course of human history."

"They have?" she said skeptically.

"Yes. Remember how the ancient city of Thebes was plagued by the Sphinx, who posed a riddle to all who passed by her: What walks on four legs in the morning, on two legs at noon, and on three legs in the evening?"

"I know!" said Isaac. "The answer is man. As a baby, he crawls on all fours. As an adult, he stands on two feet. As an old man, he needs a cane."

"Very good," I said.

"I don't know about this," she said.

"Come now, be a sport. Isaac, do you also know the riddle over which, legend has it, Homer worried himself to death? The riddle was posed by a common fisherman: What we caught we tossed away; what we could not catch we kept."

Josephine was miffed. Isaac, of course, knew the answer. Do you? Or would you have died ignorant like Homer?

Prestidigitation

I left Isaac and Josephine to their own devices and turned to the mounting correspondence. It is not uncommon for me to receive letters from amateur mathematicians who burn the midnight oil exploring the properties of numbers. This letter, however, is most unusual.

"Dear Dr. Crypton, I'm thinking of basing a religion on the number 153. The other day I was taking an all-too-bumpy taxi ride. I was trying to memorize the information on the medallion, in case I had to report the cabbie to the authorities, when I was struck by how remarkable the cab's number was. It was 153. Of course, in the Gospel of St. John, Simon Pete draws 153 fish from the Sea of Tiberias. What's so special about 153? I kept asking myself. And then it came to me. It's the sum of the first seventeen integers: $1+2+3+4+5+6+7+8+9+10+11+12+13+14+15+16+17$. What's more, it's the only three-digit number that's equal to the sum of the cubes of its digits. In other words, $1^3+5^3+3^3+$ is 153. Imagine that! But that's not all. The number likes to stay around in other ways, too. Take any number whatsoever that's a multiple of 3. Sum the cube of its digits to get another number. Now sum the cube of its digits. Keep doing this and you'll ultimately get—you guessed it—153. Sincerely yours, Euler Euclid."

This is a free country, and Mr. Euclid may base a religion on whatever he feels like. But he should not make false claims, as he has done once here. Where?

Out to launch

It's not just mathematicians who write me. I hear from all types, even astronauts. The second letter in my stack of mail was from a shuttlenaut.

"Dear Dr. Crypton, With all the soul-searching about the future of the manned space program, I thought you'd want to know what it's really like up there, aboard the shuttle.

"Although we were in space for only seven Earth days, we saw the sun rise and set more than 100 times. At one point, we used a 50-foot-long robot arm to launch a satellite and were treated to a spectacular eclipse when the satellite passed in front of the sun. The pearly corona shot out from behind it. In this shaded sky, with no atmosphere in the way, the orbs Mercury and Venus looked brighter than ever. The other astronauts gasped, and I jumped up and down. But soon, the eclipse was over, and we had to avert our eyes as old Sol ruled the heavens once more.

"We placed bets on how many of the 32,000 heat-resistant tiles would fall off the shuttle during reentry. I told my fellow crew members that we should donate our toiletry items to the Air and Space Museum for display next to John Glenn's toothbrush. We landed safely, and decided to break out the beer. The good news was that the beer was ice cold. The bad news was that we had left it three thousand miles behind. Yours in awe of space, Bud Mulligan."

Well, folks, I don't think Bud was ever on the shuttle. And it's not because I don't recognize his name but because of something he said. What?

The hot goods of einstein ferraro

The third letter I opened was from a young man who lives in the North End of Boston.

"Dear Dr. Crypton, we youngsters often don't appreciate the native wisdom of old folks. Take my grandmother—please. She has all sorts of household tricks that she learned in the old world, which, unbeknownst to her, are firmly rooted in science. In particular, she has an amazing intuitive understanding of heat. For example, on humid days she opens the oven door wide and then closes it just before she turns it on. Some of my friends think she's nuts, but the oven actually heats up faster that way.

"Of course, she always puts salt in water for pasta. That way it comes to a boil faster. During the winter, she also has this quaint practice of putting a large tub of water in the basement near the vegetables. It helps keep them from freezing. She always prefers white coffee cups because that way the coffee stays hotter longer.

"I think my grandmother knows more applied physics than I ever learned in school. Sincerely yours, Einstein Ferraro."

Well, folks, it warms the deepest recesses of my heart to see the young respecting the old. But, with all due respect, either the lady is really batty or Einstein is as dumb as he says he is.

Stupid pet tricks

I barely finished Einstein's letter when the phone rang. "Dr. Crypton," boomed the voice on the phone. It was Harrison Tweed. "I'm in Ecuador."

"Ecuador?" I said. "What are you doing there?"

"I've come to research the guinea pig."

"The guinea pig? Have you taken up medical research?"

"No, no," he giggled. "I've come to see if their pelts would make good hairpieces."

"I should have known."

"Well, doctor, I've found something much better, something that may displace you as the smartest intellect in the world."

"What? You're talking nonsense."

"No, doctor! I've discovered a brilliant guinea pig. I've saved her from ending up on a carving plate. Guinea pig is a national dish here."

"And how does she exhibit her intelligence?"

"She is a music aficionado. Play her a classical piece and she'll stomp her forepaws once if it's Brahms, twice if it's Beethoven, three times if it's Bach. She's so smart, David Letterman would have nothing to do with her. I'm going to be her agent in the States. I know we'll make millions on tour. And, doc, she's so easy to care for. All you need feed her is lettuce, celery, and barley. I'll tell you what. I'll give you a piece of her if you float me a couple grand."

"Tweed," I said, "I've had enough." How did I know Tweed was up to another fraudulent scheme?

Dreaming is for the birds

Josephine had gone off to an international women's conference in Nairobi, where she was hobnobbing with the likes of Maureen Reagan and Madonna. I was left to care for her three-year-old.

Isaac had thoroughly trashed my place. He had been through the kitchen cabinets, looking for materials with which to make superconductors. He had been through the medicine chest, looking for drugs whose chemical composition he didn't know. And he had even been through the three-foot-deep basement crawl space, looking for new species of rodents.

Finally, he had conked out. But he woke with a start. "Uncle Crypton," he wailed. "I've had a terrible nightmare."

"Tell me about it," I said in my most soothing voice. I'm not used to comforting children, but I tried my best.

"I was on the moon, you see, as part of a pioneering colony where birds were being raised. I was standing outside, all suited up, enjoying the spectacular lunar landscape. Suddenly, huge hawks—much larger than any I've seen on Earth—with little oxygen tanks strapped to their backs, swooped down and started attacking me. They flew at me from every which way, trying to peck through my suit." Isaac started to cry, and I patted him on the back.

"There, there," I said. "I can see you're dismayed but if you knew a little bit more science, you'd realize it was only a dream." What did I mean?

Darkness at noon

Isaac was relieved that his nightmare couldn't come true. He fell right back asleep, and I read a curious letter.

"Dear Dr. Crypton, Some time ago I was on a long plane flight. Next to me was a balding man with disheveled white hair and long silly sideburns. He pulled down the window shade and turned off the overhead reading light. I thought he was going to sleep. Instead, he took out a pad and started writing madly. Some nonsense about a mule that destroys an empire.

"After awhile, I introduced myself. He said his name was Isaac Asimov, and started spouting all kinds of facts and figures. He told me that for the last few miles of our trip, we would descend at an angle of three degrees. Federal regulation, he muttered. When we were taxiing to the gate, he pointed to the control tower and called attention to the slanted windows. Another federal regulation, he said. He launched into a long-winded explanation, but I was busy fixing my hair.

"That evening my husband told me that Isaac Asimov was a famous writer. I wish I had known that at the time. I would have gotten his autograph. Sincerely yours, Gail Bria."

Well, folks, either Mrs. Bria is a big liar or the man on the plane was an imposter. How can I be sure?

Venngeance

I couldn't keep my eyes open any longer. I fell asleep and slipped into a strange, complex dream world. I dreamt that I had been captured by an evil logician named Socrates Venn. After Venn tried to torture me with a series of diabolical mind benders, he offered me a choice of three rooms to retire to. "One room," he chortled, "contains a gorgeous, voluptuous lady and the other rooms contain tigers."

"So," I said, trying to maintain my composure in the face of adversity. "The odds are two to one I won't have an amorous adventure this evening."

"Not necessarily," Venn laughed. "You never know what the tiger might have in mind."

"Can you not give me a small clue as to the lady's whereabouts?"

"Of course, I almost forgot. There's a sign that goes on each door." Venn proceeded to take out three signs and tack them up.

The sign on room 1 said, "A lady is in this room." The sign on room 2 said, "A tiger is in room 1." And the sign on room 3 said, "A tiger is in this room."

I was about to charge into the first room because of the inviting sign on the door when I noticed the sign on the second door, which gave me pause.

"Haste makes waste," he chuckled.

"I need another clue," I begged.

"OK," Venn said. "If you must know, at most one sign is true."

Did I possess enough information to choose the lady with certainty?

The case of the three witches

With my captor watching, I triumphantly charged through the third door, expecting to find the lady. But instead I found another door, blocked by three small witches. "You do not play fair," I screamed at my captor.

"I do," he cackled. "She's behind the door, only you need to deal with my three friends first. I must warn you. These are strange dames. Each one either always tells the truth or always lies."

"How many of you three speak the truth?" I asked the first witch, but she spoke so softly I couldn't make out her response.

"What did she say?" I asked the second.

"She said only one of us tells the truth."

The third witch piped up: "Don't believe her," she said, pointing to the second witch. "She's lying."

"I think you've talked to them enough," said my captor. "Pick any two of the trio and tell me if each tells the truth. If you're right, you may proceed through the door to the lady."

Was I able to solve the problem?

What a woman wants

Having solved the lying puzzle that my captor posed, I made my way through the door to find the lady waiting. She was beautiful and voluptuous and had soft, sensitive eyes. I knew at once that this was the woman of my dreams.

"I want you," I said.

"Not so fast," she replied. "How do you know that I want you?"

"A legitimate question," I said. "What are you looking for in a man?"

"I want him to be healthy, wealthy, and wise."

"That's me," I volunteered.

"Perhaps, but we'll have to see. I know only four men: Agamemnon, Brutis, Daryl, and you. Only one of you fellows has all the characteristics—health, wealth, and wisdom—of my ideal man. If you are clever, Crypton, you'll see if you qualify. The four of you meet seven conditions:

1. You and Daryl are not both wealthy.
2. Each of you has at least one of the desired traits.
3. Brutis and you have the same income and net worth.
4. Only three of you are wealthy.
5. Only two of you are healthy.
6. Only one of you is wise.
7. Agamemnon and Brutis have the same degree of healthiness or sickness."

Was I the ideal man?

Behind the eight ball

I do not usually let emotions get the better of me but I smiled broadly when I realized that I fit my temptress's description of the perfect man. Nothing stood between us now except a rather large pool table.

"I'm ready," she said, chalking the tip of her long, slender cuestick.

"Pool?" I whined. "I didn't know that this was part of the bargain."

"It isn't really," she said. "I haven't forgotten that you are largely a man of the mind."

"I see."

"What I have in mind is a little intellectual exercise involving the numbered balls, all fifteen of them. The idea is to position them in the usual triangular configuration that begins a game, but do it so that each number is the difference between the two numbers above it. If you were doing this with only three balls, a solution would be:

$$3 \quad 2$$
$$1$$

For six balls there are several solutions, including:

$$6 \quad 1 \quad 4$$
$$5 \quad 3$$
$$2$$

Now, dear Crypton, do it for all 15 balls."

"For you I'd do anything." And I promptly arranged the balls into the desired triangle. What's the arrangement?

Throwing in the towel

Before my temptress and I could get to know each other, I woke up to harsh reality: Isaac Forebrain, child prodigy, was vomiting on my shoes. The three-year-old was actually aiming for my shoes because the only other possible landing area was the snow white expanse of my deep pile living room carpet. Before Josephine had departed, she told Isaac, "Don't mess up anything in Crypton's house."

"Look!" he shouted. "The carpet is still clean!"

"Isaac," I said, "I appreciate your effort, but my shoes are a mess." He ran into the kitchen and returned with a dish towel. As he bent down to wipe up the mess, I noticed a small tear run from his eye, down his cheek and plop onto the mess on my Guccis. Apparently, he was more embarrassed than he let on.

"Isaac," I said to console him, "cheer up. Before you use the towel, I'll give you a lesson in topology." Intellectual nourishment always cheers Isaac up.

"Hold the towel firmly, a corner in each hand. Now without ever letting go of a corner, tie a knot in it." Isaac tried to comply, but after rolling around the floor for five minutes, he was forced to admit defeat. I showed him the solution, which delighted him considerably. Unfortunately, the knotted towel compromised our shoe-cleaning effort. How did I make the knot?

Secrets of the orient

While three-year-old Isaac was busy programming the home robot, I caught up with my mail. The most interesting letter was from Tokyo.

"Dear Dr. Crypton, Times sure have changed. Think back to 1965 and recall your reaction to the phrase *made in Japan*. Does it bring to mind words like *shoddy*, *cheap*, and *imitation*? Now think what that same phrase means today: *dependable*, *superior*, and *high-tech*. Yet you Americans have this idea that we aren't creative, that we take your designs for cars, microchips, VCRs and do them one better.

"But take it from me: We Japanese are very creative. Why just this month at the Tokyo Idea Olympics a team of inventors exhibited the Next Wheel, an improvement on the motor car. It runs not on wheels but on four Chinese woks mounted horizontally on the ends of vertical axles. When the woks are spinning, the car remains stationary as long as the axles are perfectly vertical. Tilt the axles ever so slightly and the vehicle moves. Now that's creative.

"But there's more. We have umbrellas that fold up with the wet side in, so that they don't drip. And umbrellas whose hollow shafts are filled with sand; at the push of a button the sand is ejected so that you don't slip on icy sidewalks. We have underwear safe deposit boxes, square melons, special sneaker-only washing machines, double-headed pay phones so that two people can get on the line, and toilets in which the tank doubles as a sink. Now that's innovation. Sincerely, Yoichi Toyota."

Well, Mr. Toyota has strayed from the straight and narrow. One of the products he touted doesn't exist in the land of the rising sun. Which one?

A scrambled affair

When Josephine returned from the Nairobi women's conference she was filled with a renewed sense of purpose and faith in her gender. She had exchanged all her paper currency for Susan B. Anthony dollars and plastered her living room with portraits of Hypatia of Alexandria, a legendary female mathematician who was brutally murdered by a fifth-century mob. Josephine had decided to become a lavatory architect in order to redress a classic inequity between the sexes: women must queue up to use a public restroom, whereas men seldom have to wait in line.

When Josephine came over to pick up her three-year-old prodigy, Isaac and I were deep in enigmatic conversation.

"Desperation," I said.

"A rope ends it," Isaac shouted.

"Crypton! What warped thoughts are you putting in my child's head?" Josephine said. "I've only been away a week and you've corrupted him."

"No, no, Josephine," I said, "listen closely." I turned to Isaac: "Southern California."

"Hot sun or life in a car," he instantly answered.

"The lost paradise," I said.

"Earth's ideal spot," he said.

"The United States of America," I said.

"So much in a tea fee started it," young Isaac responded.

"Stop this nonsense!" Josephine shouted.

It's not nonsense at all. Why?

Coming of age

While Isaac and I continued playing anagrams, Josephine wrote a feminist critique of science fiction. She had just finished a section calling for more little green women and fewer little green men.

"Crypton," Isaac said, "I know so little about your family."

"What is it that you want to know?" I started to fidget. Like Gary Hart and Pat Robertson, I too have skeletons in my closet.

"I know you have a sister," he said. "And I know about your nephew, Carl 'Killer' Crypton. But do you have any nieces?" The question seemed innocuous enough, and I saw it as an opportunity to test the tyke's analytical powers. "I have three nieces, Isaac, and the product of their ages in years is 36."

"Very funny, Crypton," replied the sniffling three-year-old. "But you haven't given me enough information to determine their ages."

"Perhaps not. Well, the sum of their ages is your house number."

Isaac snorted. "You still haven't given me enough information."

"I don't suppose I have. One of these days you'll meet my nieces. My favorite is more than a year older than the others."

Josephine stirred. "Crypton," she said, "can't you just answer Isaac?"

Well, I had. What are their ages?

Booked any good reds lately?

I don't know how Josephine did it. She had been back from Nairobi only a day before she managed to rope me into babysitting not only Isaac but also Boris, his red-diaper-baby friend. Like Isaac, Boris is exceptionally brainy for his age. He's a chess master, a budding ballet star, and can recite from memory all three volumes of *Das Kapital*. Isaac and Boris spent a quiet evening poring over maps of the Urals and downing caviar from Josephine's private stash. Then they got into animated discussion.

"I cannot wait," said Boris, "until the Soviet Union sets another duration record for manned space flight. Imagine what it must be like up there to look out and see the stars twinkle. The cosmonauts are heroes."

"Ha!" said Isaac dismissively. "That will be the day."

"How dare you insult the Soviet space program!"

"It is you whom I insult. You know nothing of space."

"To insult me is to insult the Communist state. To hear you speak like this, Lenin must be rolling in his grave."

"Ha! You are just a blabbering idiot. You know as little about Lenin as you know about astronomy."

I had to intercede before nuclear war broke out between the two boys. But Isaac was right twice over. How?

Utter nonsense

Josephine had been nagging me for weeks to take her and Isaac on a vacation at the shore. I had been putting her off because I didn't want to take time out from my studies of dinosaur extinction. But finally I broke down and consented to take a day off. The shore was too far for a day trip, so I proposed a rowboat outing in a neighbor's pond. Josephine grumbled but agreed.

Isaac packed a picnic lunch, Josephine took along Jane Fonda's new workout book, and I brought a sack full of promising rocks from the Late Cretaceous.

Even before we got into the rowboat, the conversation turned to what the young chef had packed for lunch. Isaac pulled out a huge platter of steak tartar. It looked like there was five pounds for each of us.

"Holy cow!" Josephine said. "You know I'm a vegetarian. And beef isn't good for you."

"Eat beef to reduce the greenhouse effect and save the planet," Isaac shouted.

"My boy's going insane," Josephine wept. "It's all your fault, Crypton, for tormenting him with mathematical brain teasers."

I smiled because there was some method to Isaac's seeming madness. What?

A weighty problem

The pond was mossy green, and the water level showed no signs of the winter's drought. Indeed, the pond was filled to capacity, the water even with the land.

As soon as Josephine, Isaac, and I stepped into the boat with our possessions and pushed off, the water overflowed ever so slightly onto the land. All three of us are fervent conservationists, and so we found the wasted water to be unacceptable. Josephine suggested returning to shore and making the boat lighter by leaving off some of the cargo. Isaac, who even at the tender age of three thinks life is too short to retrace one's steps, proposed dumping my rocks into the pond.

"That will never work," said Josephine. "Throwing the rocks in will make the water rise even more." The boy and his mother got into a loud, weighty argument. Lost in the discussion was the fact that I might not like my rocks dumped into the pond, even if it was for a good cause. But putting that aside, was Isaac's suggestion helpful?

I am curious yellow

Josephine Forebrain was still obsessed with the idea that belching cattle are in part responsible for the pernicious greenhouse gasses that have accumulated in the atmosphere. "Where do those cows think they were raised?" she asked. "In a barn?" All the talk of gaseous Guernseys made me eager for dinner, and so the three of us jumped ship and headed to the supermarket.

I like nothing better than shopping for food, and Isaac evidently feels the same way. The three-year-old was running up and down the aisles, looking wide-eyed at the wealth of gastronomical choices.

"How about some cephalopods?" Josephine asked, pointing to a box of frozen squid.

"I'm more in the mood for univalves," Isaac responded. He fetched a can of conch.

"Too expensive," Josephine said. "I'm afraid we must settle for a dinner most foul."

Isaac laughed at her clever pun and rushed off to the poultry section. When we caught up with him, the pudgy child was on a stepladder, studying the fresh chickens in the display case. "Here's a good one," he said as he plucked a plump juicy bird from the case and handed it to his mom.

"Why Isaac," she said, "you've chosen a particularly nice one. Look how yellow its skin is. That means it has extra flavor and surface fat. It probably grew up outdoors, bathed in the light of the sun."

The trip to the supermarket was getting to me. Josephine was revealing her naiveté. How?

The case of the balanced meal

We went from the supermarket directly to Josephine's house. I still couldn't get over the fact that three-year-old Isaac was a master chef. Surely the tyke would slip up somewhere in the preparation of the evening meal.

After preprandial chitchat I headed into the kitchen. Isaac was standing on a chair so that he could reach the counter. He was slicing cheese.

"What have we here?" I inquired.

"It's England's famed Cheshire. I had it flown in just for you. No one else is able to make it like they do."

"Why's that?"

"It's the Cheshire soil. It imparts a unique flavor to the grasses that the cheese cows eat."

"I see," I said. "And what's the main course?"

"*Farfalle with fungi.*"

"*Farfalle?* I haven't heard of it."

"It's a butterfly-shaped pasta. I'm making a delicate sauce with dried wild mushrooms."

The child certainly sounded like a gourmet, although the whole time he was sipping not a glass of wine but a glass of milk. Josephine picked up the milk carton and inspected the label.

"Why Isaac, you healthy boy," she said. "This milk is 96.5 percent fat free. You're so smart to develop good eating habits at your age. Low-fat milk is the way to go."

Isaac blushed and started to prepare the pasta water.

I blushed too. "Not everything about this meal is kosher," I said. "I'm afraid you don't know everything about food. There's been a little slip." What?

Sailor's delight

Josephine was not pleased that I had refuted her rosy assessment of Isaac's milk consumption. To cheer herself up, she pried open a box of imported Swiss chocolate.

"Candy is dandy, but liquor is quicker," said little Isaac. "At least Ogden Nash thought so." For a three-year-old, the breadth of his literary knowledge was incredible.

"Do you really think liquor is quicker?" Josephine inquired.

"Is the pope Catholic?" I replied. "Of course, liquor's quicker. Science proves it. As soon as alcohol reaches the stomach, it's absorbed directly into the bloodstream. The sugar in candy can't be absorbed until it moves beyond the stomach to the small intestine."

"I'll still have the chocolate, thank you," Josephine said, not wanting to admit that she had been defeated by my superior intellect. Isaac, however, raced past her and grabbed the candy.

"The early bird gets the worm," the tyke shouted gleefully.

"It certainly does," I said. "There is certainly an advantage to avian punctuality. Birds are more likely to catch worms early in the morning because that's when the ground is coolest and the worms are closest to the surface."

"You're just a big showoff," Josephine protested.

"No," I replied, "I'm just a man of science."

Isaac peered out the window; the sky had a reddish hue. "Red sky at night," he peeped, "a sailor's delight."

I smiled because there was wisdom in the mariner's adage. What's the wisdom?

A bad case of tunnel vision

Josephine's trip to the neighbor's pond didn't assuage her need to travel; it merely fueled it. She'd been complaining for months that I never went anywhere with her. Finally I gave in, and against my better judgment I accompanied her and Isaac to London.

Josephine wanted to see for herself whether Charles and Di's marriage was really on the rocks. We hung around outside Buckingham Palace for hours in a cold drizzle and never got a glimpse of the royal couple. After three days of this nonsense, I convinced Josephine that we should go out on the town.

We rented a Jaguar and, after a few false starts on the right side of the road, headed into the tunnel that runs under the Thames. As our luck would have it, a lorry jackknifed in the middle of the tunnel. No one was hurt, but there we were stalled under the river.

The couple in front of us had the right idea. The man got out, carefully spread his Burberry coat on the pavement, kicked off his oxfords, and sat down on the coat. The woman, carrying a big wicker picnic basket, joined him. She opened the basket and took out two steak and kidney pies and a bottle of Dom Perignon. When he removed the cork, it barely popped.

"It's probably flat," Josephine said, gloating.

"Sour grapes!" I said. "At this moment, any drink would be welcome, even vinegar."

Suddenly, Isaac dived over the seat, landing between the two of us. The tot started pounding on the car window, trying to attract the attention of the picnickers.

"Don't disturb them, Isaac," Josephine said. "You don't want them to think that we're rude Americans."

But Isaac ignored his mother's exhortations and banged away.

"Isaac!" Josephine shouted, as she swatted him, "what's come over you?"

"Mommy," he cried, "I'm trying to help.

What was the boy up to?

The river's rude surprise

After half a day under the Thames, a towing crew and a squad of bobbies had managed to remove the disabled lorry, freeing us from the stagnant air of the tunnel. As soon as we found a suitable parking spot along the river, we pulled over and got out to enjoy the fresh air. A barge passed, followed closely by a ferry and then a scull. The coxswain was shouting "Stroke! Stroke!" as the oarsmen paddled in unison like a finely tuned machine. Josephine smiled and I squeezed her hand. A look of panic crossed her face. I dropped her hand and started to apologize for my forwardness.

"It's not you," she interrupted. "It's *that*." She covered Isaac's eyes with one hand and with her other hand trembling, pointed toward the boat's wake. There bobbing at the surface was a clothed, skinny corpse.

"'Tis a bloody shame," boomed a voice from behind us. I spun around, and was face to face with a cigar and a large, pear-shaped man in a trench coat. "Havana Gold," I said.

"Close," he said, exhaling a cloud of smoke. "Monte Christo." Josephine was turning pale and pasty. And Isaac had buried his head in her hemline.

The man waved his cigar in the direction of the corpse. "Good thing you weren't here an hour earlier. You'd have seen him jump in and drown himself. He was a broker. He lost half his net worth on Black Monday, when your stock market collapsed." The man shook his head. "This is not a pretty sight, certainly not for women and children. It's not what you came to London for. It's like something you'd see back home, on *Murder, She Wrote*. I tell you what. Why don't you leave your car here for awhile and come with me?" He gestured toward an Excaliber. "I'll drive you around town and show you a fine time."

"No, thank you," I said.

Why did I decline Fatso's kind offer?

Moonlighting

We were certainly not having a great holiday. Stuck in front of Buckingham Palace, trapped under the Thames, witness to a bobbing corpse—that's not exactly my idea of a fun time. We tried to recover with a rousing dinner of fish and chips and a big evening at the theater, Josephine's favorite form of entertainment besides the unwholesome pleasure she derives from tormenting me. Afterwards, I immediately fell asleep in my room at the Savoy, but in the middle of the night I was awakened by a loud rapping on the door.

"It's me, Josephine."

"Josephine," I said, unbolting the door. "What's the problem?"

"Come, at once. Isaac is having another lunar nightmare." I went with her down the dimly lit hall until we reached her room. There Isaac was, cocooned in the bed covers, trembling.

"Tell me your bad dream," I said.

"Well," he whimpered, "I was on the moon again, in that experimental colony. I decided that I'd leave the building and go for a walk so I got all suited up. No sooner was I outside when a huge man in a suit appeared. He shouted 'Monte Christo' and started to come after me. I was terrified and ran for my life."

"Monte Christo?" Josephine said.

"Why," I said, "that's the cigar the weirdo by the Thames was smoking."

Isaac's face emerged from the covers. He looked somewhat relieved.

"You'd be completely relieved," I said, "If you realized your dream is scientifically impossible."

What did I mean?

When rain comes between mother and child

Josephine and Isaac and I were in London's Hyde Park, checking out the soap-box speakers. Josephine was taken with a woman named Miss Anthrope, who was calling for an end to harmony among races. Isaac was listening to a Shaw scholar giving an impassioned lecture on *Pygmalion*. I was intrigued by a Michael Jackson look-alike, who was telling the crowd how bad he was. Suddenly, it started raining and the three of us scrambled for cover under a large, leafy tree. Still, we were getting quite wet. A dapper man walked by, and Isaac ran out and tugged on his pants legs, begging in his high-pitched squeal: "Bumbershoot? Bumbershoot?"

"Come back here, Isaac," Josephine shouted. "Why must you spew nonsense at a time like this?"

"Bumbershoot! Bumbershoot!" he continued.

"Idiot, come here!" she shouted even louder. I cringed; she'd eventually pay for her anger in psychotherapy bills for Isaac. The three-year-old did return, the shower from the sky joined by the tears from his eyes.

"Let's go to the car," she said.

"It's only three blocks away. We can run."

"I'm going to walk," he said defiantly.

"Nonsense," she said. "You'll get much wetter if you walk." Josephine sprinted off and Isaac held his ground, walking.

Is Isaac really such a bad kid?

The case of the slimy stranger

I did not like the look of things. A strange, animated man was handing Isaac chocolate and gesturing toward the youngster's chest. Perhaps such encounters are common in London, but it gave me the creeps. I rushed over and scooped up the child.

"Didn't anyone ever tell you not to take candy from strangers?" I asked.

Before Isaac had a chance to answer, the stranger spoke: "I meant no harm. I'm a herpetologist. I was merely pointing to the alligator on the boy's shirt."

Why, I wondered, did Josephine insist on always dressing him up in those preppy Lacoste outfits? The boy, after all, is only three.

"A herpetologist, how interesting," I said, trying to disguise my suspiciousness.

"Yes," the man said. "My specialty is the alligator—a reptile that is making a comeback in your country. You are from the Colonies?"

"Yes, we are."

"In your Southeast, alligators are now so common that they're sometimes more than a nuisance; at least thirteen people were attacked in Florida last year, one of them fatally."

"How gruesome," I said, although I must admit I was repelled not so much by what the man was saying but by the man himself.

"Oh, no," he said. "They are charming beasts. They hibernate during cold weather. They have broader snouts than crocodiles. By the way, it is crocodiles that are gruesome, not alligators."

I shuddered. "I'm afraid, Mr. Herpetologist, that you don't know your alligators from your crocodiles." What did I mean?

Spaced out

Josephine and I were wrapping up our stay in London. When I checked out of the Savoy, the clerk handed me a letter that bore a Soviet stamp. I eagerly ripped it open, only to find it was from the huckster par excellence, Harrison Tweed.

"My dearest Crypy, I hope this letter reaches you in your far-flung travels. I too am abroad, taking advantage of the age of *glasnost*. I'm going to Moscow to present Gorby with a hairpiece that covers his burgundy birthmark. But first, as a guest of the government, I journeyed to the Kazakhstan, where I watched the Soyuz space capsule land on the snow-covered steppes. Cosmonaut Yuri Romanenko emerged smiling, returning to Earth after a record 326 days in space. Family and officials congratulated them. As I gave him a bear hug, he jokingly told me that future spacemen would be better off with bald heads to avoid haircuts, six big arms, and legs with grips on them to keep steady. I wish you were here to share in the celebration. Best regards, Tweed."

I put down the letter in disgust. Tweed was up to his old trick: stretching the truth. What's wrong with his story?

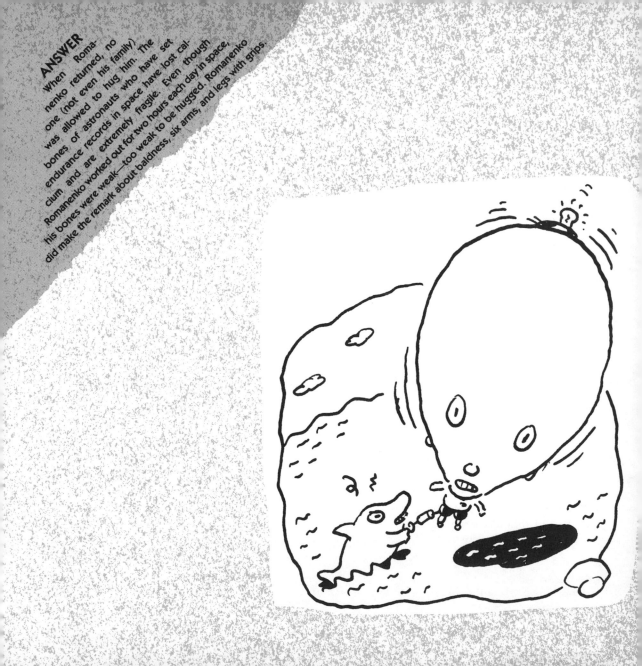

Fishy nightmare

Josephine, Isaac, and I were huddled together in the center section of a 747, trying to catch some shut-eye as we flew home from London. Suddenly, the three-year-old awoke with a start, his brow dripping with sweat.

"Isaac, what's wrong?" Josephine asked, scooping the child to her side.

"Mom, I had another terrible nightmare."

"Not again," Josephine said. "What did you dream?"

"I dreamt I was swimming in the ocean. All of a sudden I heard a medley of weird noises—clicks, squawks, chirps, quacks, whistles, and raspberries—and then a sleek fish shot by me. I wasn't scared, just a little disoriented. But then it returned. It was a dolphin. It was even quite friendly looking. I was going to pat it, when I heard a squealing noise behind me. I turned around, and was face-to-face with another dolphin, only this one had an evil grin. It charged, impaling me on a long hypodermic needle." Isaac started to cry.

"It's O.K.," I said, patting the boy's mop of hair.

"No," said Isaac. "The worst part is yet to come. The needle was connected to a carbon dioxide cartridge, which discharged its gas, pumping me up until I just exploded."

"Oh, Isaac," said Josephine, "you've always had a vivid imagination." She turned to me: "Now, Crypton, calm Isaac down by saying what you always say when he has a terrible nightmare: 'Son, you wouldn't be so scared if you realized the substance of your dream was scientifically impossible.' "

I shook my head sadly. "I'm afraid, Josephine, that I can't say that this time around."

"What?" she said.

"The dream could well be true," I said, "except that Isaac still has a thing or two to learn about dolphins."

What did I mean?

The case of the runaway microwave

Our descent into Kennedy was uneventful. The top of the plane did not blow off and all the engines continued to function. Since I had been out of the States for so long I decided to throw a little dinner party for my friends and intellectual sparring partners. I was particularly looking forward to seeing Ron C. Plute, the well-known psychoanalyst, and Hector Pomic, a fellow paradoxologist. The names of both men are anagrams of the way they look.

At my parties the same thing always happens. I whip up some light dish; everyone eats it, gets smashed, and tries to humiliate the others at a variety of board, card, and mind games.

While I waited for my guests, I put a circular cornbread cake into the microwave oven. For the cake to taste best, it would have to bake exactly nine seconds. Unfortunately, the oven timer was broken. The only other timers I had were a seven-second hourglass and a four-second hourglass. Was I able to use them to bake the cake?

Also, what do Ron C. Plute and Hector Pomic look like?

Visitors from the red planet

While the cornbread cooked, I reviewed a diary entry from October 30, 1938—"The Day the Martians Landed"—that I received in the mail from a gentleman in New Jersey.

"Today was quite exciting, although a bit of a letdown. I had finished my homework early so I turned on the radio. The announcer described how these creatures from Mars had landed in a huge metal cylinder on a farm near Grovers Mill. The army surrounded the spaceship, but the creatures fired deadly heat rays and advanced in huge fighting machines. I ran into the living room where dad was sipping a beer and reading the sports pages and told him the news.

" 'Joyce,' he called into the kitchen. 'You never should have given Rick that spaceman costume for Halloween. This flying saucer stuff really goes to his head.'

" 'But dad,' I said, 'This stuff is real! It's on the radio.'

" 'This is real, too!' he shouted, and swung his hand to swat me. I ducked and ran back to the radio. By then the state militia had taken over the station and was ordering everyone to evacuate. My mother joined me, and started to weep when the announcer said, 'They're taking New York.'

"Dad appeared in the doorway. 'Joyce,' he said, 'Why the hell are you listening to the radio when there's dinner to be cooked?'

" 'This is for real, Tom,' she cried. 'We should pack sandwiches and get out of here.' Far off we heard a siren wail. Dad, too, finally looked upset, but a few minutes later we found out it was only a radio play. Dad was annoyed, mom was relieved, and I was disappointed."

Well, folks, how do we know that this "diary entry" is as fake as Orson Welles's radio hoax?

The case of the enigmatic inscription

The corn bread was ready, but still the party guests had not arrived for a festive evening of stimulating mind games. So I put a Buddy Holly record on the stereo and retired to the study to catch up on my mail. Although the holidays had long passed, greeting cards were still dribbling in from obscure parts of the globe where the mail service hasn't yet made it into the twentieth century. The first card, from an observatory on Antarctica, showed exuberant extraterrestrials jumping around on the surface of a multicolored orb; the caption read, "Greetings from Uranus." Another card, from a linguistic institute on an island in the Maldives, was blank except for the enigmatic inscription, "ABCDEFGHIJKMNOPQRSTUVWXYZ." I chuckled out loud, until my mirth was derailed by the chime of the doorbell.

It was the beautiful and brainy Josephine and her three-year-old prodigy, Isaac. "Come in," I said, bowing and gesturing toward the 3D chess set in the living room. "It's wonderful to see you."

"Doctor," Josephine said, "don't be so effusive. You and I both know that all the money I have on me will be yours before the evening's over. You and your little devious games and bets."

"Come now Josephine," I said, but I stopped in mid-sentence because the stereo suddenly went off. I rushed over to it and peered in its innards. "Drat! A microcircuit has fused. We won't have any music for our party."

Isaac raced over to the phone and started madly pushing the buttons, first 3212, then 333, then 222, then 399, then 3212, then 333, and finally 22321. Josephine and I watched in astonishment.

"Knock it off," Josephine yelled at the tyke. "No phone number is that long!"

"I'm only trying to help," Isaac said, tears rolling down his rosy cheeks.

And, by golly, he was. How? (Also, what did the enigmatic Christmas card mean?)

Just dessert

My guests had arrived and so I took the corn bread into the living room to serve to them. I was about to cut it into four equal pieces with two knife strokes when Hector Pomic stopped me. "Dr. Crypton," he said, "by cutting big pieces you're maximizing the possibility that someone won't finish her cake. It would be better to cut the corn bread into eight pieces. That way each of us can eat two pieces if his appetite holds up. But if someone is full after the first piece, his second slice will be available for the rest of us to eat."

"You have a good point," I said. I pictured the circular cake neatly divided into eight slices. I wanted them to be perfect, so I practiced by moving the knife up and down above the cake in the four places I intended to cut it.

"Dr. Crypton?" Ron C. Plute said somewhat hesitantly.

"Yes?" I replied.

"It's a wasted effort for you to make four incisions. You can divide the cake into eight pieces with only three cuts."

"Thank you. You're quite right," I told him. With the tip of the knife I traced out on the top of the cake the places where I'd make the three cuts.

Lora gulped. "Don't cut it that way. You're making the pieces different sizes."

I was mortified when I realized that she was right. In a second, however, I was able to cut the cake three times and get eight equal pieces. How did I do that? And how did I intend to make the cuts before Lora had corrected me?

As it turned out, all of our ingenuity was for nothing because we each ate two slices. A few cocktails later, the four of us were eager to start playing the evening's games.

An olympic lie

With the stereo broken, Isaac was still making music with the Touch-Tone phone. Josephine was all smiles now that she recognized that 011 (pause) 12369# was "Yester-day." Isaac started on another tune when he was interrupted by the doorbell. It was none other than Harrison Tweed.

"Doctor! It's great to see you," Tweed boomed as he slapped my back.

"Tweed, it's been awhile," I said, trying to disguise my contempt for the fawning toady.

"Indeed, it has. I've been traveling. I spent some time in Calgary."

"Calgary, Canada?"

"Yes. I went to the Olympics. I figured I could sell hairpieces to the swimmers with shaved heads."

"Swimming isn't an event in the Winter Olympics."

"Precisely what I discovered, Doctor. So I went and watched the luge, the only Olympic sport timed to one-thousandth of a second."

"Is that so?"

"Yes, it's so exhilarating how fast they move on those sleds. Bonny Warner had great form, her stunning sixth-place finish the best ever by an American in singles competition. At the finish line I had the chance to be up close and personal with her, shaking her hand after the finish before her sled had even come to a complete stop."

"Enough," I said, "You're up to your old tricks. You've lied again." How?

Picking up the pieces

"I'm afraid, Doctor, that I can't stay. I was just dropping by to say hello. I've a long day ahead of me tomorrow." With that remark Harrison Tweed adjusted his fake moustache and headed for the door.

"Not so fast," I called after him. Although I do not particularly enjoy Tweed's company, I do enjoy taking his money with my fiendishly clever bets.

"Doctor, I really must go. I must be alert in the morning."

"Alert? For what?"

"For Bobby Fischer."

"The chess player? The kooky world champion who ousted the Russians and then defaulted on a rematch?"

"Precisely the man. I'm going to play Fischer tomorrow."

"But he's a top-notch player. And you're just a lowly wood-pusher."

"Doctor, you underestimate me. I'm a strong player. In fact, I even beat Fischer once, in Rio in 1969. I remember the game vividly. Bobby opened by thrusting his king pawn forward two squares. I countered, and we soon found ourselves playing a Max Lange Attack, specifically the Fried Liver variation."

"I was three pawns up in the early middle game, but Fischer launched an aggressive flank attack. I rebuffed the assault, and then kept swapping pieces. When the dust cleared from the board, I saw that he was down to just his bare king. I had only my two knights left and, of course, my king. Boy those horses galloped, driving his poor king into the corner where I decisively mated it."

Tweed was out of breath. But his excited delivery didn't keep me from realizing that this story couldn't possibly be true. Why?

Games people play

Tweed," I said, as the lobbyist for the South Korean toupee industry headed toward the door, "you are obviously drunk. Otherwise, you wouldn't have told me the tall story about Bobby Fischer."

"How dare you accuse me of being drunk!" Tweed responded. He was tugging nervously on his hair.

"Look," I said, "You're a compulsive liar. Normally your tall stories are clever, the lie being well-concealed. The Fischer story was feeble. That's why I know you're under the influence of an excess of spirits."

"Pooh! Pooh! Pooh!" Tweed exclaimed. He tugged so hard on his hair that his toupee went flying.

"Your response only proves my point. You're hardly being your eloquent self."

"Nonsense. I'm as coherent as a laser beam. Look here, at this tick-tack-toe game I just won." He unwadded a piece of paper and displayed the scribbling:

$$
\begin{array}{ccc}
X & 0 & 0 \\
0 & X & 0 \\
0 & X & X
\end{array}
$$

"If I were inebriated," Tweed added, "I wouldn't have been able to win against so formidable an opponent as young Isaac."

Three-year-old Isaac had gone to bed. Tweed knew that I wasn't going to wake the child in order to check out his story. But without Isaac's testimony, I knew that Tweed was lying yet again. How did I know?

Six—legged folks

By the time Isaac woke up, all the guests had left and I had finished cleaning up the debris from the party. It was a beautiful day, and Isaac and I decided to go for a walk in the local forest preserve. "Look Crypton!" the enthusiastic three-year-old shouted, pointing to a slender, sticklike insect perched on a fallen tree. "It's a praying mantis."

"Indeed, it is. Why it even has its head raised and its front legs extended in an apparent attitude of supplication."

Isaac bent down for a closer look. "I think it's the common Chinese mantis," he said. I'm always amazed by the tyke's intimate knowledge of flora and fauna.

"You are right, my lad," came a strange voice from a thick grove of bushes. Out stepped an elf of a man carrying a small butterfly net and a jar with cotton in the bottom. "It is the Chinese mantis, or more accurately *Tenodera aridifolia sinensis.*"

Isaac looked at him quizzically. "I see you're puzzled," the man responded. "I'm an entomologist. I know all about the ways of the mantis. It's an avid carnivore."

"Ah," I said, "so it really should be called a *preying* mantis."

"You're a wit, my friend. Is it OK if I tell the boy about the mantis's sex life?"

"By all means. He knows more about sex than I do."

"Well, mantis sex makes *The Devil and Miss Jones* look like a family movie. You see, just before copulating, the female ritualistically bites her mate's head off. Headless, he can still mate. Afterwards, she devours the rest of him. Entomologists have known of this odd behavior for more than half a century."

"You're quite entertaining," I told the stranger. "But I think that you're no entomologist at all." Why?

Is there room for cuteness in this world?

Confronted with my knowledge of the Chinese mantis, the elfin stranger readily conceded that he was not a card-carrying entomologist, although he had dabbled in the subject decades ago in junior college. "Bugs are not really my thing," he said, putting down his butterfly net and extending his hand, first to Isaac and then to me. "Gore's the name—Mort Gore—and gore's my game."

"I'm not sure I follow," I said. "But I like a man who's an enigma."

Mort leaned forward conspiratorily. "I have an uncanny talent for uncovering the dark, disturbing side of things."

My palms began to sweat. I didn't know where the conversation was heading and whether it was appropriate for a three-year-old. Isaac, however, was paying no attention; he was crawling around on the forest floor, herding ants toward a log.

"Come, Isaac," I said, taking hold of the child's hand. The two of us walked silently for a mile or two, with Mort trailing us. I had hoped to lose him, but even with his bad limp, he was never more than a few steps behind.

The forest ended abruptly, and we found ourselves on a flat, expansive prairie. "In the distance," said Mort, breaking the silence, "I'm sure there are prairie dogs. They *seem* so cute, living in towns, kissing and nuzzling and grooming each other. But, take it from Gore, things are seldom what they seem."

"Please, stop," I told him. "Don't tell the child the prairie dog's deep, dark secret." What's the secret?

The twisted tale of mort gore

Isaac and I still hadn't managed to lose the creepy, fraudulent entomologist as we strolled across the abandoned prairie. Luckily, however, Gore refrained from telling us more disturbing stories about cute, cuddly animals. But before we could part company, we were thrown together by adversity.

"Look!" Isaac wailed, his eyes bulging with fright. A black twister, sucking up dust, was approaching from the distance. I scooped up the three-year-old and ran toward the house. His adrenaline surging, Mort limped after us at an especially brisk pace.

"Head toward the basement!" I shouted over my shoulder as we entered the house. "That's the safest place."

"You're right," said Mort, hobbling up the front steps. "But first we must throw open the windows."

"That will do us in! That will do us in!" Isaac shouted.

"Calm yourself, child!" Mort said. "Opening the windows is what you're supposed to do."

Who was right?

The case of the roasted rodent

Huddled in the basement, we survived the tornado. True, there was one close call, when a windowpane blew in and bopped Mort Gore on the head, rendering him unconscious. But he soon woke up and shared with us the nightmare that had raged through his dazed mind.

"It was awful," said Gore. "You know I'm a devout Roman Catholic of the old school. In my nightmare, it was Friday during Lent, and I was somehow stranded in desolate grassland in Venezuela. A herd of capybaras, the world's largest rodents, some weighing 140 pounds, charged by me and dived into a lake. They squealed and frolicked in the water. Soon, men on horses galloped by and lassoed a few of the oversize rodents. The cowboys made a fire and roasted a capybara. A particularly depraved-looking man, with a toothless smile, forced me to eat his portion. I was disgusted because ordinarily I refrain from meat during Lent and eat fish. Luckily I regained consciousness before the dream could get any worse."

"Well," said Isaac, "that hardly seems like a nightmare. You did nothing wrong."

"Has the child gone mad?" Gore shouted at me.

Has he?

The dream that boomeranged

Having exposed Mort Gore's dream, Isaac was clearly pleased with himself. But he also looked agitated.

"What's wrong?" I asked.

"Like Gore," Isaac said, "I too passed out when the twister sped by. I'm not sure why. I don't think anything hit me."

I examined the tyke's head, and found nothing out of the ordinary. "You look OK," I told him.

"I was frightened. I had another one of those nightmares about being on the moon."

"Tell me about it."

"Well, I was going stir crazy in the cramped quarters of the experimental work station. So I got all suited up and headed out for a walk. I had barely made it past a few boulders when a man jumped out. Through his visor, I could see the evil look on his face. He carried some kind of weird gadget—three balls on the ends of cords."

"That gadget is a weapon called a bola." I said. "Primitive tribes here on Earth use it to hunt. It's interesting that bolas have reached the moon."

"Yeah, sure. It's very interesting. Well, I didn't like the look of it—or of him. I started to run. He lost no time running after me. He also had a boomerang."

"Ah, another primitive hunting device."

"He threw the boomerang up in the air. It wasn't aimed directly at me, but, knowing that boomerangs curve, I was afraid it would ultimately hit me. At that moment I woke up in a cold sweat."

"Have no fear, Isaac. Your dream, as always, is scientifically impossible—something you should keep in mind next time you're having a nightmare."

What did I mean?

Damn lies

"Mort," Isaac said, "we don't know anything about you. Do you have a family? Or were you hatched?"

Gore laughed. "Of course I have a family. I'm from Virginia. Fredericksburg, to be precise."

"What's it like there?" the tyke asked.

"There's a beautiful river called the Rappahannock. It's an Indian word meaning *quick rising waters.* To control the flood waters and produce electricity, the white man has built a huge dam 194 feet high and 8,850 feet long."

Isaac looked skeptical. "What you say is all very interesting but also a bit odd."

"What do you mean?" Gore said.

"Well, if you asked me about my home town, New York City, I could tell you how wonderful the Empire State Building is, but I wouldn't be able to tell you its precise dimensions." The three-year-old certainly had the analytical powers of a man ten times his age.

"Perhaps you couldn't," Gore chortled, "but I could. Beauty is in the details. If you don't believe the height and width I recited, look up the Rappahannock in the *Britannica.*"

"I think I will," said Isaac. The boy fetched the encyclopedia and found the river. "I apologize," he said. "It says right here that the Salem Church Dam is 194 feet high and 8,850 feet long. You must have grown up there."

"Your apology is accepted. The community was so proud of the dam that the schoolmarms drilled the dam's dimensions into us."

"Gore," I said, "for all the fibs you're telling the boy, your nose should be 8,850 feet long." How had he lied?

Eastern wisdom

Even in the basement, as I tried to forget about the twister, I could not get a moment's peace. My wireless phone rang.

It was Harrison Tweed. "I am in Bangkok, the City of Angels," he said.

"You certainly left town fast. What are you doing there, Tweed?"

"I'm here on business."

"Business?"

"Yes, I've convinced the Thais that the 160-foot statue of the Reclining Buddha near the Royal palace would look much sharper with a hairpiece."

"You want to put a toupee on Buddha? Surely, that's sacrilegious."

"Times are changing, Doctor, even here. Western music is replacing classical dance. Many of the canals that once made Bangkok the 'Venice of the East' have been replaced by wide roads. Traditional dress is giving way to Western clothes. Why not a change in the Buddha's pate?"

"This time, Tweed, even you have gone too far."

"But think of it, Doctor. There are more than 50 million Thais, and a hairy Buddha would make them more receptive to wearing toupees."

"Tweed, I really doubt . . ."

"Sorry to cut you off. But my hosts are waving chopsticks. That must mean dinner. Yum! My first authentic Thai meal. Good-bye, Doctor."

But before Tweed could hang up, I told him that I doubted he was in Thailand at all. Why did I doubt his story?

Big apple census

Tweed apologized profusely for faking the story about Thailand. "I was just trying to keep your mind active," he explained. "Actually, Doctor, the real reason I'm calling is just to hear your voice. I read in the paper about the tornadoes out your way, and I wanted to make sure everything was OK."

"Everything's just dandy," I said, "if your idea of OK is sharing a basement with a needy tyke and a hobbling creep who's an encyclopedia of all things dark and disturbing." I glanced over at Gore, and he was smiling evilly, his head bobbing.

"Well," said Tweed, "there's nothing like a little intellectual nourishment to distract you from your troubles."

"Talking to you is hardly my idea of intellectual nourishment."

"Don't get testy now. I'm in New York City, doing a little market research on hair styles. I presented the ex-mayor with a toupee, which he sorely needs, and he told me two astonishing statistics. First, there are more New Yorkers than there are hairs on the head of any one New Yorker. Second, no New Yorker is completely bald, although the ex-mayor is rapidly approaching that. Here's where I need your help. Does it follow that two New Yorkers must have exactly the same number of hairs?"

Could I help Tweed, assuming I wanted to?

Gore shows his hand

I did solve Tweed's little hair problem, and he thanked me heartily, promising to send me his latest wig. I put down the phone and peered out the narrow basement window.

"It looks like it might be a full moon," I said.

Gore started to drool. "Good," he said. "It means that lycanthropes will be out."

"What's a lycanthrope?" Isaac asked.

Gore's mouth foamed uncontrollably. "It's a werewolf," he said.

The three-year-old started to shiver. I admit that I, too, was a bit nervous.

A dog barked in the distance. I let my imagination get the better of me, and the bark became a howl.

"Don't be scared, child," Gore said. "There are ways of dealing with ordinary werewolves. It is the werewolf king you should be afraid of. Everybody is afraid of the werewolf king."

Gore really knew how to be reassuring. Isaac looked pasty. He buried his head in the tail of my trench coat.

"But you're in good hands," Gore added, "because the werewolf king is afraid only of me."

Isaac's head emerged from my coattails. The boy started screaming and raced out of the basement. Why?

If I've taught you anything, dear reader, it's that life itself is the strangest lie. Just stick to the straight and narrow. Expose prevarication no matter where it may lead you. And keep in mind that the check is rarely in the mail. Do as I say and it won't hurt a bit. Yours in pursuit of truth, Dr. Crypton.